TALKING ABOUT I

Six interchurch discussion booklets based on conversations worldwide

BOOKLET FIVE

On whose authority?

G. R. Evans

THE CANTERBURY PRESS NORWICH

The Canterbury Press Norwich, St Mary's Works,
St Mary's Plain, Norwich, Norfolk NR3 3BH

The Canterbury Press Norwich is a publishing imprint
of Hymns Ancient & Modern Limited

ISBN 0 907547 61 3

First published 1986

© G. R. Evans

Printed in Great Britain at the
University Press, Cambridge

A booklist

Christian communities have lately been talking to one another on seveal fronts. You can find an account of the way these dialogues began and a summary of what they have achieved so far in *Anglicans in Dialogue* (Church of England Board for Mission and Unity, 1984), and of others in *Growth in Unity* (see below).

Abbreviations used in these booklets

BEM   *Baptism, Eucharist and Ministry.* Faith and Order Paper 111. World Council of Churches, 1982.

ARCIC   *The Final Report of the Anglican–Roman Catholic International Commission.* SPCK/CTS, 1982.

AL   *Anglican–Lutheran Dialogue: the Report of the European Commission.* SPCK, 1983.

AR   *God's Reign and Our Unity: the Report of the Anglican–Reformed International Commission.* SPCK/St Andrew Press, 1984.

AO   *Anglican–Orthodox Dialogue: the Dublin Agreed Statement, 1984.* SPCK, 1984.

Resp.   *Towards a Church of England Response to BEM and ARCIC.* CIO, 1985.

You can buy a collection of *Reports and Agreed Statements of Ecumenical Conversations on a World Level*, ed.

H. Meyer and L. Vischer (World Council of Churches, Geneva, 1984), called *Growth in Unity*.

The Bookshop, Church House, Dean's Yard, Westminster, London SW1P 3NZ, can supply all these by post, or your local bookshop can get them for you if you want to read the Reports for yourself.

5. *On whose authority?*

What is Christian authority?

Today we value our freedom of thought and action and we do not take kindly to the idea of authority.

But Christian authority is not dictatorial or domineering (Resp. 220). It is not imposed on us whether we like it or not. It is something we contribute to and support and which depends on our response to make it authoritative over us.

If you put your foot in your doctor's hands, you are giving him authority to treat it. You let him do what he thinks will make it better. That may mean taking orders from him. He may tell you to plunge it alternately into very hot and cold water. You yelp as you do it, but you do not resent his orders. You do it under his authority and at the same time of your own free will.

Authority can be freely and willingly experienced, and in no way a tyranny.

God is unimaginably powerful. Yet he gives his children freedom to challenge him.

If you put your foot in your doctor's hands

In Christ he took the form of a servant and suffered. It is this power of the crucified that is lodged in the Church.

So the power of God is exercised in enabling his creatures to respond to him freely. He comes to us on our own terms. He does not force us. He invites us (Resp. 216).

But because of his power he is able to provide a secure framework for us to be free to love him and be ourselves.

That is the pattern of all Christian authority.

The Bible and the Church

How does God's authority make itself known to us?
How do we recognise that it is God's authority?
What means do we have of responding to it?

There are two main sources we can look to if we want to know what God would want us to think or to do.

One is a reference book: the Bible.

The other is a living thing, which we ourselves are part of: the Church. It is because we are ourselves members of the Church that we share in the working of Christian authority in the world.

The Bible and the Church can never be separated, and they were never meant to be thought of apart from one another.

The Church must always base its teaching on the Bible and follow the Bible in its worship and common life because the Bible contains the witness of the apostles to what God did in Jesus. It is the record of the authentic foundation of the faith (ARCIC, Authority 1. 1; Resp. 214). It gives the account of Jesus' teaching and of his life which was handed on by those who heard and saw him. That makes it the most important source of information we have.

Yet the Bible itself comes from the living proclamation of the Church. That is obvious everywhere in the Acts of the Apostles and the Epistles. The formation of the collection of texts which make up the Bible (the 'Canon') took place within the Church's experience of worship, as the Church lived and taught the Gospel and gave thanks to God (ARCIC, Authority, I, Elucidation, 2; Resp. 214).

From the primary authority of Jesus, then, comes not only the authority of the Bible as a written record (we can go back to whenever we want to be sure we are believing and acting as his people should) but also the authority Jesus gave to his 'body' on earth, the Church. These are not two authorities, but one:

(*a*) because they both depend on Jesus' authority, and

(*b*) because they are intimately dependent on one another.

The Church can never ordain anything which is contrary to the Bible's teaching, or add to the essential truths it contains. But it has the responsibility of acting as guardian century by century, handing on the Bible safe and unaltered to future generations of Christians. In the first Christian centuries when copies had to be made by hand it was easy for mistakes to get in and be passed on in other copies. Today you can go into any bookshop and see the success of this guardianship in the Bibles on the shelves.

The Church also acts as a witness.

The first 'witnessing' produced the Bible itself, as the result of some very direct action by the Holy Spirit, and the work of the apostles.

The Church's witnessing since has involved not adding more truths but unfolding the Bible's teaching so as to make more and more of the truths it contains understood. The tests of its witnessing are whether it is in accordance with the teaching of the Bible itself, and whether it is speaking the mind of all Christians under the guidance of the Holy Spirit. Although Councils and Popes have given formal expression to this witness, that is not what gives it authority. The authority comes from God himself, making his truth known by the agreement of the faithful in every generation, helping them to realize it step by step and to get it clear. This sacred 'tradition' or 'handing-on' by the Church is carried in the minds and hearts of believers everywhere.

Reception

This process of judging by the whole Church over long periods of time – by all God's faithful people in every age – is called 'reception'. The Church 'receives' its understanding of the faith by actively thinking about it and discussing (See Booklet 1.)

In a Bible study group the members help one another's understanding and act as a check if anyone suggests an interpretation which would be out of keeping with sound faith. That is a small-scale example of the process of 'reception' at work. When you get it right you recognise that, and everyone accepts the answer.

What you are doing now in your discussion group is part of this 'receiving'.

It is vital to bring your ideas together with those of other Christians, to share in the process of grasping and accepting with the whole Church, or 'reception' cannot work. It cannot meet the test of acceptance by 'all Christians at all times everywhere' in any other way.

There have been subjects on which the minds of Christians have not apparently been in agreement at all times. These are the topics ecumenical discussion is working on now, to see whether there really is disagreement or merely mutual misunderstanding, and to try to come to a common mind.

Divisions in the Church are declarations of independence. Each separated group of Christians is claiming to be able to run its own affairs under God. But to refuse to share in Christian witness with the whole Christian community is to deny what the Church is.

When your ecumenical discussion group talks about

authority it is doing one of the most important things it can to help unity forward.

Speaking the Church's mind

When a council (or primate) has articulated the faith of Christians in an area under dispute, that definition (if true and correct) is sure to be received by true believers. Reception is not what confers authority on a statement. The authority which makes something right is God's not man's. The Church's task, in all its members, is to recognise what is true and authoritative, and to find a way of saying it. But the *sensus fidelium* or 'mind of the Church' is often arrived at more or less inarticulately, because it is akin to an intuition, and at some point it needs to be written down as a formal statement which everyone can refer to. It has to be put on record.

In the early Church the 'rules of faith' which became the creeds took shape in that way. Individual congregations had slightly different forms of words but they all made the same confession of faith. In the fourth century general Councils were able to agree the exact words of the creed we now call 'Nicene', after the Council of Nicaea of 325, which made a draft of it.

The Reports of the discussions which are going on between the churches now are part of this process of putting a statement on record. Our responses to them take the process a stage further. Eventually the Church as a whole will be able to speak its mind in a form everyone can recognise and agree.

How does this happen?

Who speaks in the name of the Apostles now?

The apostles were able to speak of Christ as people who had met him and known him. But as the first generation of Christians became a second and a third generation, some way had to be found to go on witnessing without them.

A collection of books and letters was brought together and agreed upon for reading aloud in worship and for use in teaching (The Bible.)

New ministers were chosen to carry on the apostles' work. (Read the Acts of the Apostles 6. 1–6, 14. 21–23, 15. 22–28; and other passages on some of the ways this happened).

Rules of faith and later the creeds were framed to provide a clear statement of true faith which new Christians could make when they were baptised and all Christians could join in in worship, to affirm their faith afresh.

All these were ways in which the Church could safeguard the faith and hand it on to future generations.

There is still a need for it to do so.

We live our lives in day-by-day interaction with the demands of the world.

What new problems have you been brought up against lately?

Have you always known how you ought to act?

We need guidelines for a world in change. We need help in understanding how to live our faith in new circumstances. There is a constant lively tension in the Church's life as we look for principles and guidelines for our present situation. There is not always a clear-cut text from the past to answer the problems of today, and the general principles in the Bible have to be applied by the Church with the Holy Spirit's help (Resp. 237).

Read:

Romans 16. 17.
1 Corinthians 5. 1. 1–2
1 Thessalonians 5. 14.
1 Timothy 5. 20.
1 Timothy 6. 3.
Titus 2. 15.
Titus 1. 13.
Titus 3. 10.
Revelation 2. 2, 14, 15, 20.

To judge from these and other passages, three kinds of difficulty needing decisive leadership seem to have cropped up early on in the life of the Church.

(1) Problems of Church discipline, settling disputes, dealing with persistent wrongdoing – small matters but very common.

(2) Decision-making about matters of faith.

(3) The making of arrangements for choosing ministers and running the Church.

Jesus knew that his disciples would soon come up against the problem of disagreements amongst themselves (read Matthew 18. 15–18). Human beings who try to work together in a cooperative way frequently do.

Have you run a house for a family?

Have you organised an outing for a club?

Have you had to take the lead in a crisis?

How have people responded to your authority?

What have you learned from such experiences about leadership?

Has it worked better if people asked you to take charge?

Jesus advised his disciples what to do when they quarrelled. He told them to try first to make peace quietly between themselves. If that failed they were to make a more formal matter of it and ask a few others to act as witnesses. If that failed, they were to bring the

matter before the whole community. If the person who was in the wrong would not then admit it and be welcomed back into the community, they would have to give up. He would have broken away from them.

Sheep without a shepherd

That is a model for the Church in every age. Problems should be sorted out locally if possible, in the congregation where they arise. But if that does not work, they should be brought before the Church community of the area, and then, if necessary, before the whole Church.

When we look for authority to resolve our difficulties, then, we should begin by looking to one another in the Christian community, and if necessary put our problem before the whole Church.

But that requires practical organisation. At first the leaders of the community were known as 'bishops' or 'priests' without much difference being made between the two words. They presided at the Eucharist and looked after the members of the congregation as shepherds. But during the first centuries there emerged leaders of groups of communities in an area, who had responsibility for 'oversight' for them all. The Greek word for 'overseer' is *episcopos*, which we still use in 'episcopacy' and other words connected with bishopric.

As Christianity spread in the early centuries, gradually there emerged 'prominent sees', whose bishops had responsibility for several bishoprics and their bishops. The patriarchs of the Orthodox Churches are an example of that pattern in use today, as are the archbishops of the Anglican communion.

This development shows that the Church felt a need as it grew for coordinators and guardians of its work and witness, who would keep it together as one Church in faith and worship and common life.

Authority grew up in this way from the local churches to a single bishop who had 'oversight' over the whole Church, a universal authority. It came to the bishop at the 'top' from Christ through his people. It was not an authority imposed on them from above. Everything ought to be decided within the local congregation if possible, but if there is difficulty there is someone to turn to who is able to take a view on behalf of the whole Church (Resp. 220).

It has remained like that ever since. Only if the highest leadership fosters the *koinonia* by helping all bishops in their task of apostolic leadership both in their local church and in the universal Church can it exercise its 'oversight' properly. It fulfils its purpose by helping the churches to listen to one another, to grow in love and

The Queen opening a General Synod of the Church of England

unity, to strive together towards the fullness of Christian life and witness. It respects and promotes Christian freedom and spontaneity.

Is there solid ground today for affirming that the fullness of the Church's being requires there to be a special bishop

(i) endowed with a responsibility for uniquely authoritative teaching at the highest level for all Christian people, and

(ii) for the exercise of discipline and order throughout the universal Church?

All bishops have to look after their regional church, and they all have a responsibility to care for the universal communion of which each Church is part. The primate is a special case of this care for universal communion.

Alongside this emergence of a special bishop, and inseparable from it, there went another development. Bishops began to meet together in regional councils to share experiences and problems on behalf of their congregations. Their decisions were accepted as having authority because they spoke for their people, and so they expressed the 'mind of the Church', the *sensus fidelium*.

The special bishop spoke for the bishops and priests and deacons and all the Christian people in his care as they expressed their faith through this machinery of council meetings.

The question for us today is still the same. How is the Church to keep together as one and speak its mind? What ought to be the balance between councils and synods and meetings and the work of those with responsibility for pastoral care as bishops or leaders of the community? Is there still a place for a universal primate who has a special care for the Church as a whole? Someone who can exercise 'a presidency of love and an authority of service to unity' (Resp. 237)?

There are two strong reasons for thinking so, apart from the argument from the history of the Church's development. Jesus gave Peter a special task in the Church, which would clearly be necessary long after

Peter himself was dead, the more so as the Church grew bigger. The 'Petrine office' goes on being needed.

The Church is both invisible and visible. The Holy Spirit's care for the Church as a whole keeps it safe. But as a visible communion in the world it needs a leadership everyone can see and turn to.

Is the Pope Infallible?

An aspect of primatial authority in Roman Catholic understanding which causes both Protestants and Orthodox Christians particular difficulty is the idea of Papal infallibility. There is often misunderstanding even among Roman Catholics about what this means.

All Christians agree that the term 'infallibility' can be applied unconditionally only to God. 'To use it of a human being, even in highly restricted circumstances, can produce many misunderstandings' (ARCIC, Authority, I, 19).

It is the Holy Spirit who has kept the Church's teaching safe and protected it infallibly from error. Whatever its weaknesses and failures the Church can never lose its essential character nor fail to reach the goal God has given it, because the Holy Spirit makes it 'indefectible'. That does not mean 'without defects', but it does mean that it can never lose its way in teaching the essential truths of faith (Matthew 16.18).

The whole Church is given responsibility for keeping the Church's teaching free from error, by testing it against the teaching of the Bible, and by taking care to express it exactly and truthfully. This is the teaching authority of the Church (*magisterium*).

In its teaching the Church maintains the truths of faith it was given at the beginning. It puts them in the language of today. It explains them. It deals with questions and objections. But it does not add anything. In Roman Catholic as well as in Anglican understanding of the Church's teaching authority, there is no power to create new truths or to add to the faith, only to clarify and safeguard.

In teaching or declaring truths of faith, the Pope is not set apart from the universal Church as if he had special authority to say more than the Church as a whole can say. When he speaks *ex cathedra*, that is, formally as pastor of all Christians, on matters of faith and morals, he is privileged to be a single voice declaring what the Church has found to be its common mind through its councils and through thousands of discussions and contributions by Christians everywhere. The reliability of what he says is that of the whole universal Church, and that is given it by Christ because it is his Body.

This idea was first stated by the first Vatican Council (1869–70), which was intended to continue the series of universal or ecumenical Councils held in the first centuries of the Church. So it was a conciliar decision, a decision of the Roman Catholic Church speaking through its general council, that the Pope's statements in rare circumstances and on such matters should be regarded as protected from leading the Church astray.

To Discuss

A mixed record?

If history suggests that it is to Peter's successor that Christ has given the special ministry or universal oversight of the Church, that does not mean to say that Popes have always exercised the gift as they should.

There is no straight line from 'Thou are Peter and on this rock I will build my Church', to the sort of thinking found in the medieval Popes who claimed 'plenitude of power' over all things on earth.

Does the fact that a job has not always been done well mean that there is no job to be done?

The reformers of the sixteenth century rejected the authority of a universal primate in breaking away from the Roman Catholic Church. Was their action something we should now see as a historical event in response to the circumstances which have now changed? Or was it an assertion of an essential truth of Christian faith?

We are sure that it must be God's will for the Church to be one in its faith and worship and common life. Is that a practical possibility unless someone has a special responsibility to oversee and take care of universal unity in faith, worship and common life?

What reservations have the Protestants in your group had in the past about accepting primatial leadership?

Can the Roman Catholic members help?

Practical decision-making

The Church has authority to settle controversies of faith and to lay down patterns of worship and to direct its common life.

It gets its authority from Christ its head and it exercises it through the fellowship, the *koinonia* of the body of Christ, in Councils and through the leadership of the ordained ministry.

How does that work in practice?

Human beings are not good at acting together as a group unless someone organises things. Have you ever been in a crowd of people at a road accident? There is confusion and muddle until someone takes charge and sends one person to telephone for an ambulance, another to stop the oncoming traffic, someone else to fetch blankets, and so on.

The person who takes charge sets up a temporary structure or organisation, within which individuals can be useful and effective (the whole crowd cannot get into the telephone box together).

The Church needs structures in the same way, if it is to do its work effectively.

We can't all get into the telephone box

It needs to be
    organised for action
    organised for worship
    organised for making decisions about the faith when it is challenged.

Practical problems about authority, and the whole question of what authority is, have not yet been seriously tackled in the World Council of Churches' discussions. Only Anglicans and Lutherans have been working on it, in their dialogues with the Roman Catholic Church.

We need to look at all the structures and systems of organisation we have inherited and ask:
    Are they useful?
    Do they work?
    Can we make them better?